MONGORIA
Sketch Coloring Book

BEST IN TRAVEL 2017

-

TOP 10 COUNTRIES YOU DO NOT MISS IN 2017
(Volume 7)

Anthony Hutzler

Sketch Coloring Book

A view from the Trans-Siberian train at Ulaanbaatar , Mongolia

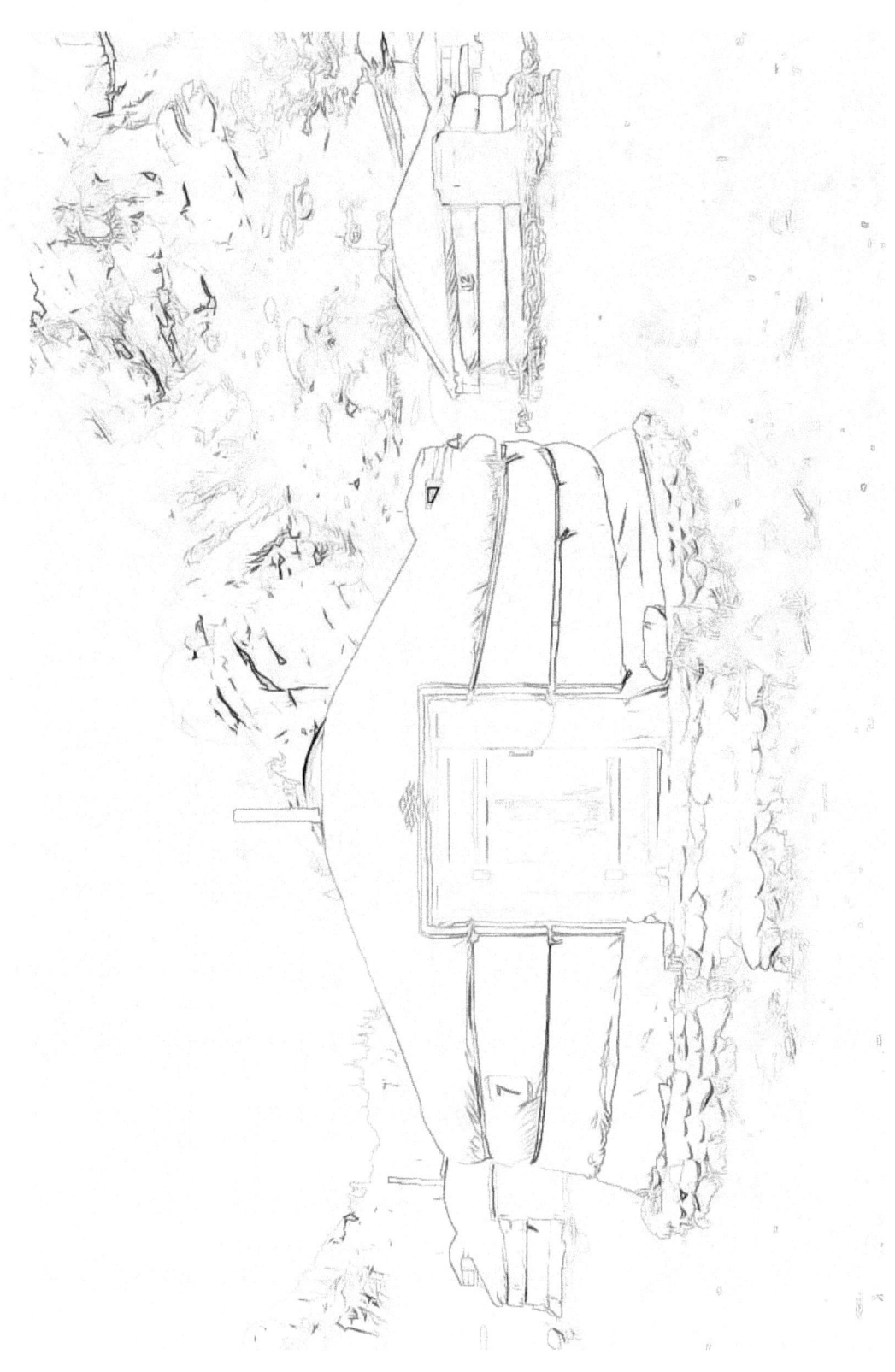

Mongolian yurt other ger in a grassland landscape

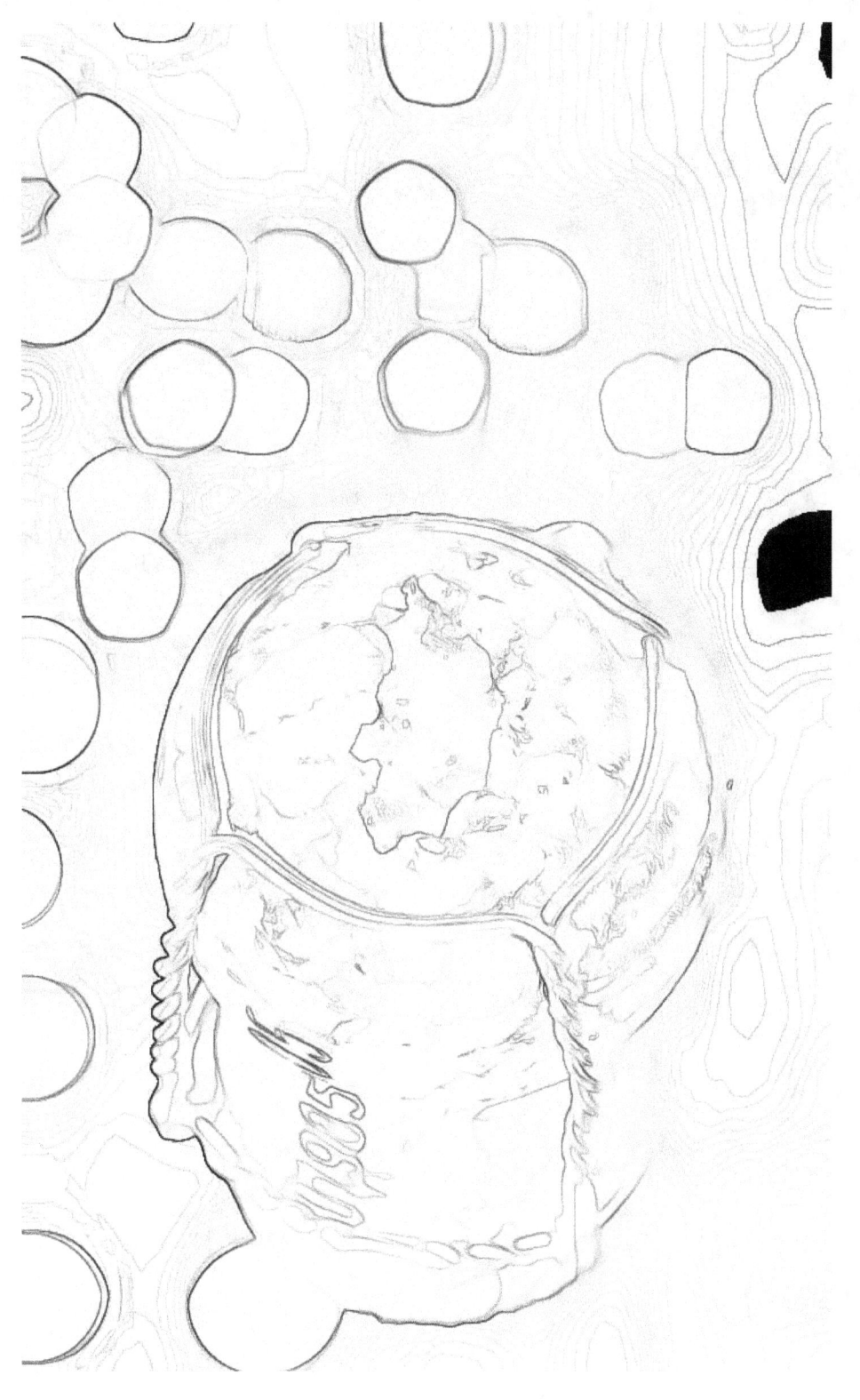

Champagne cork with the shape of Mongolia burnt in and colorful blurry lights in the background

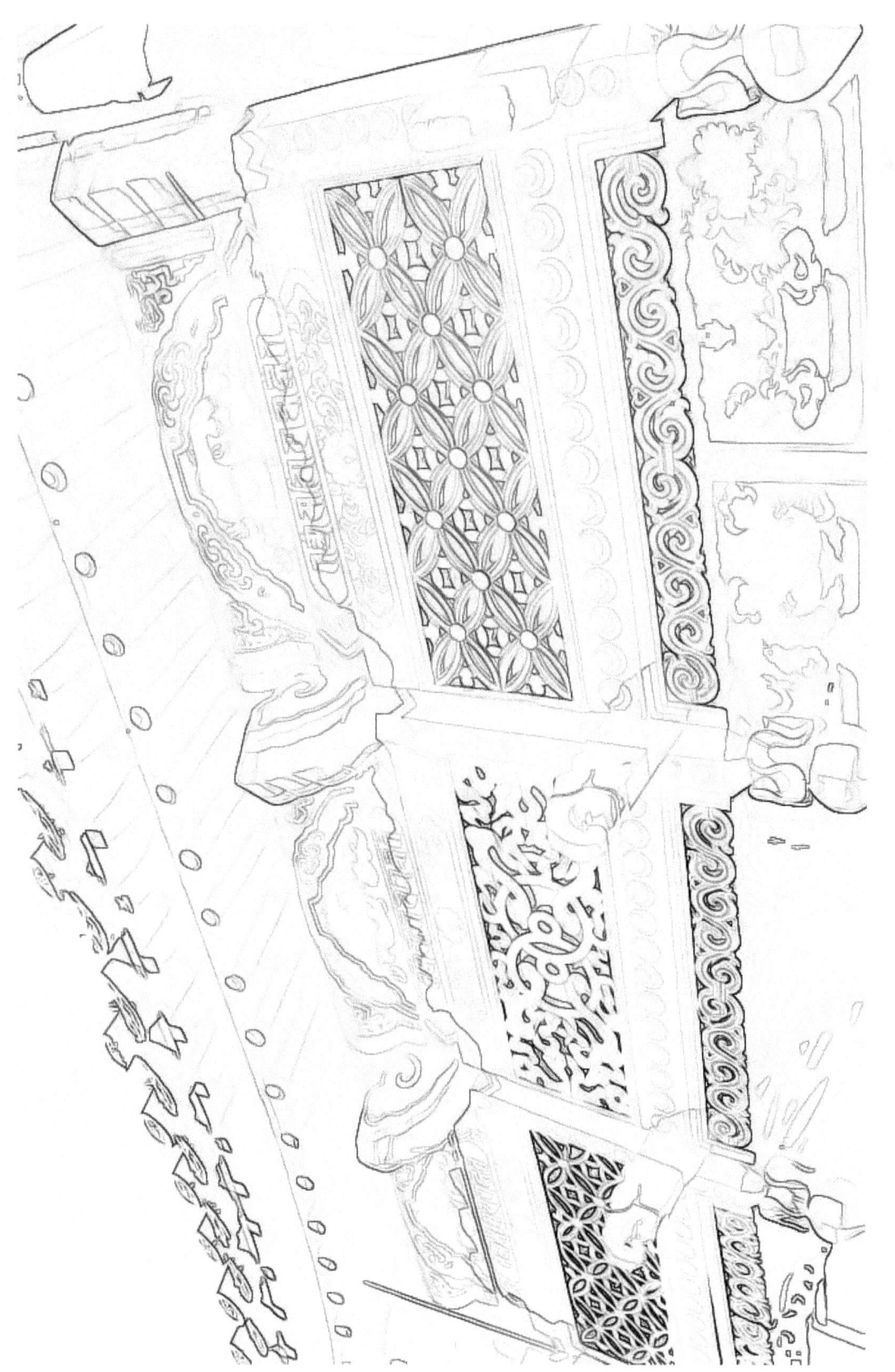

Buddhist temple in Mongolia. Datsan

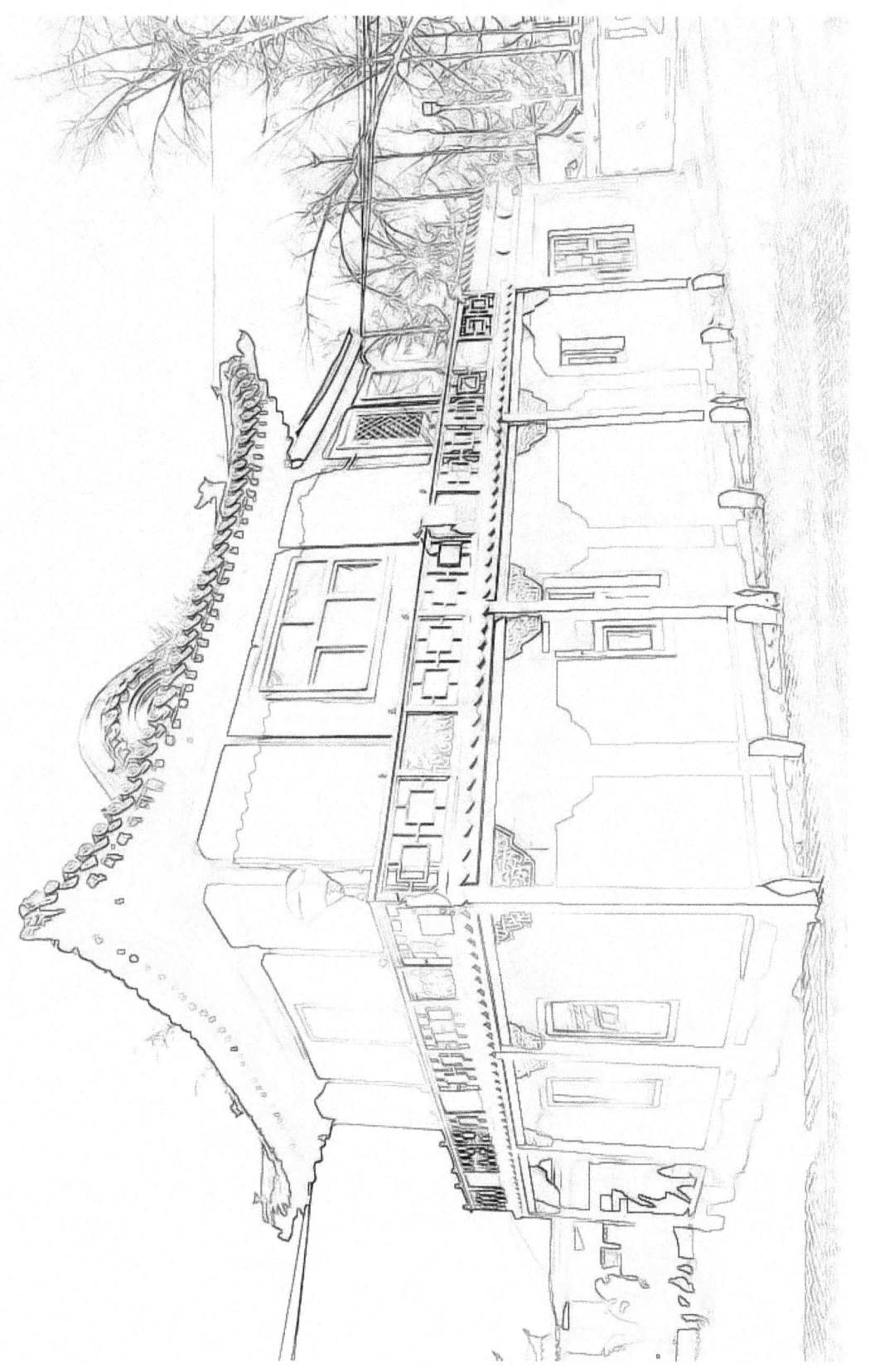

Buddhist temple in Mongolia. Datsan

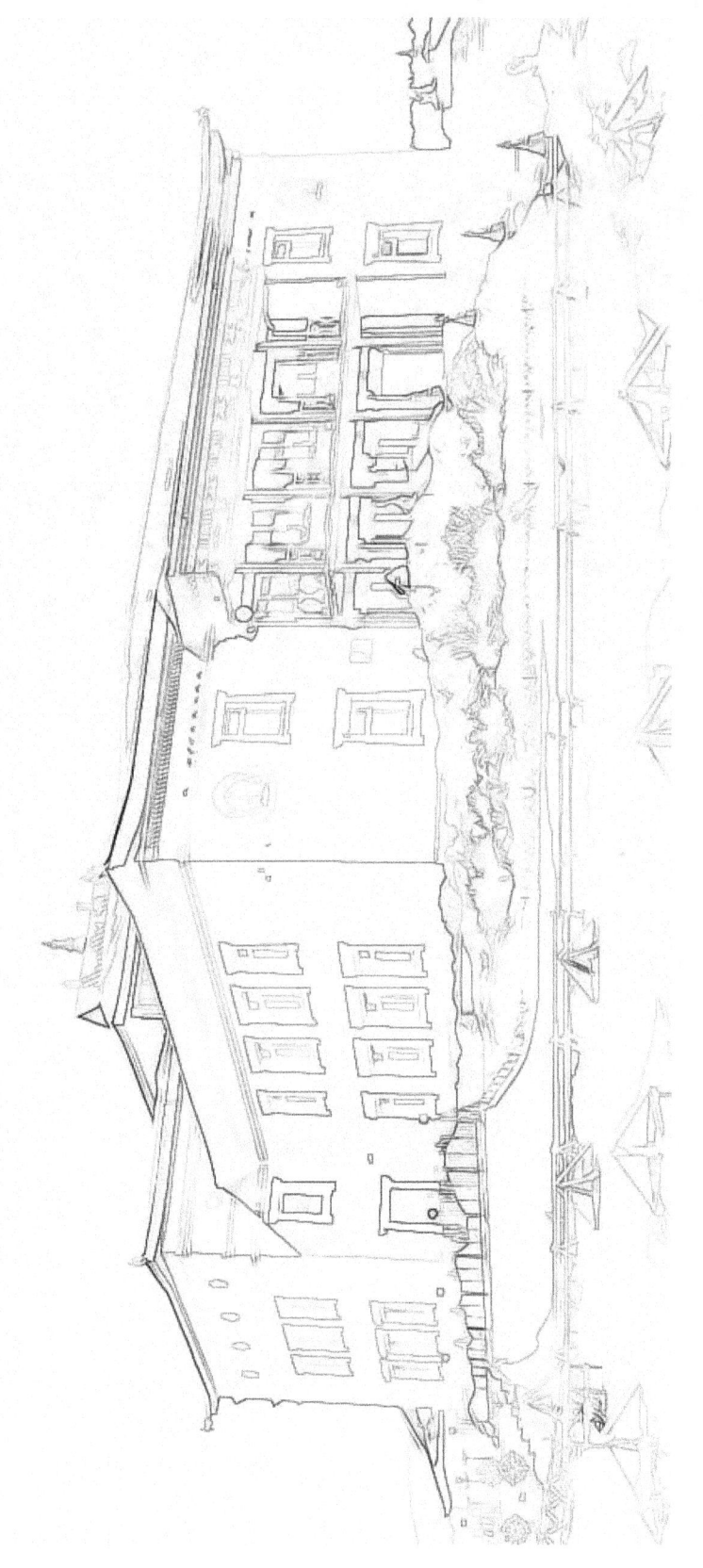

Buddhist temple in Siberia. Datsan

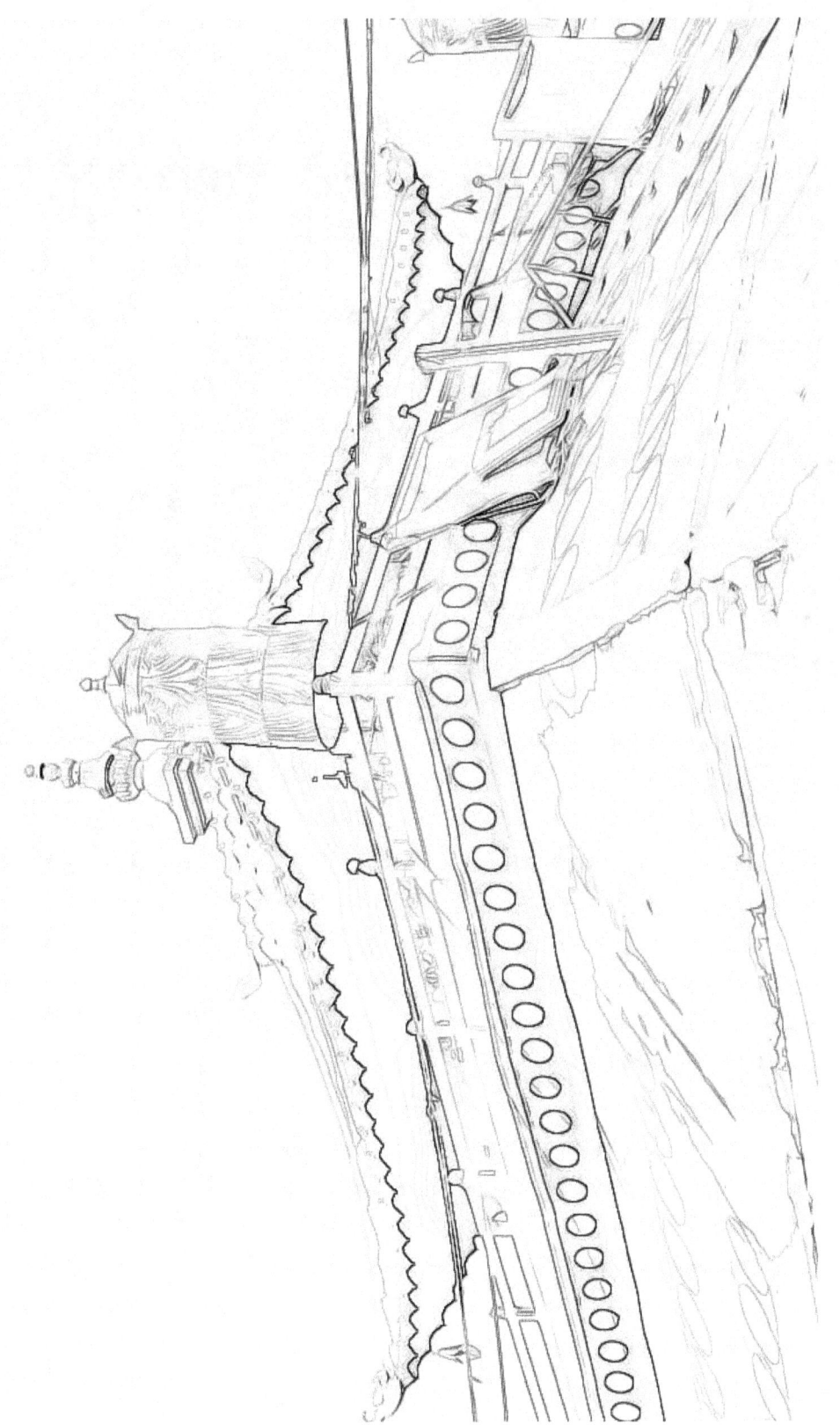

Buddhist temple in Mongolia. Datsan

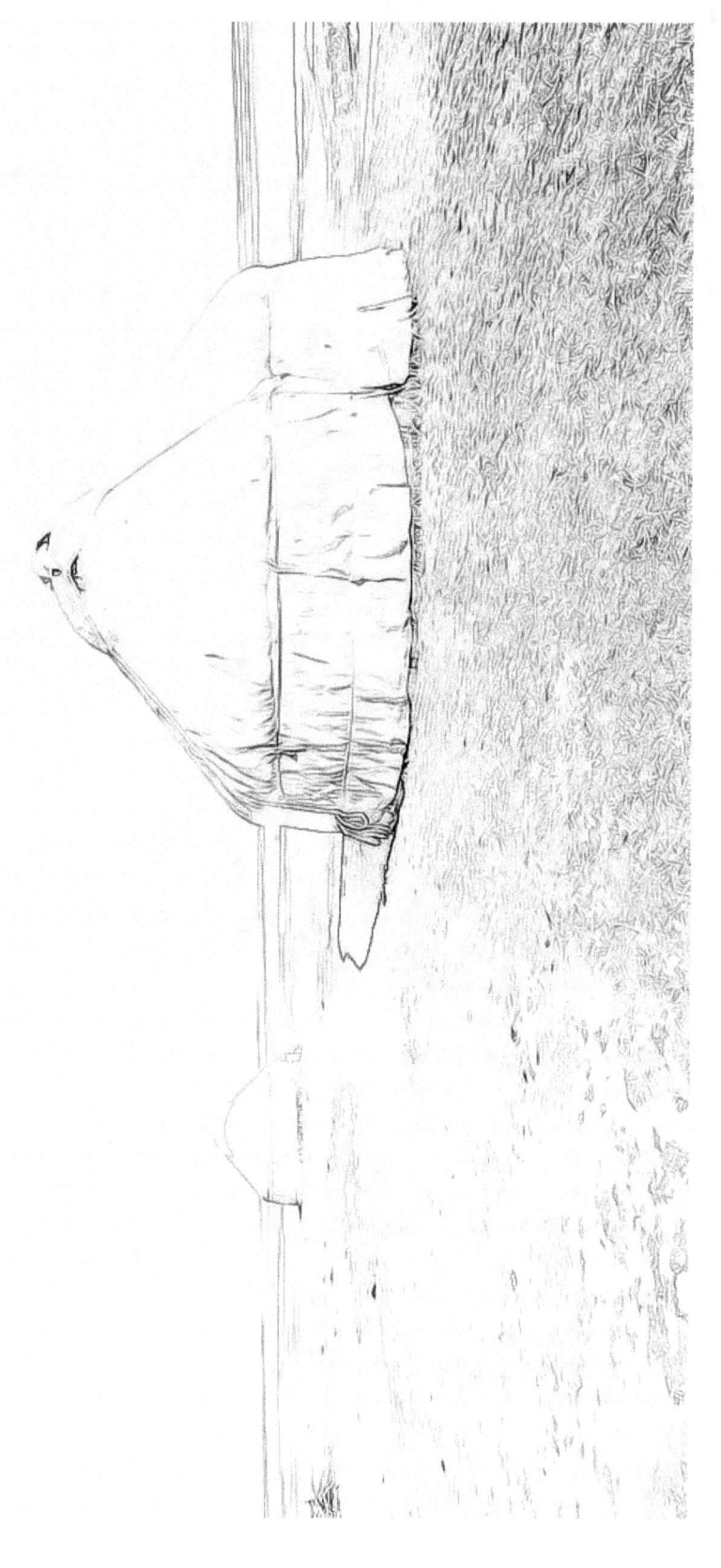

Yurta- traditional dwelling of xinjiang people

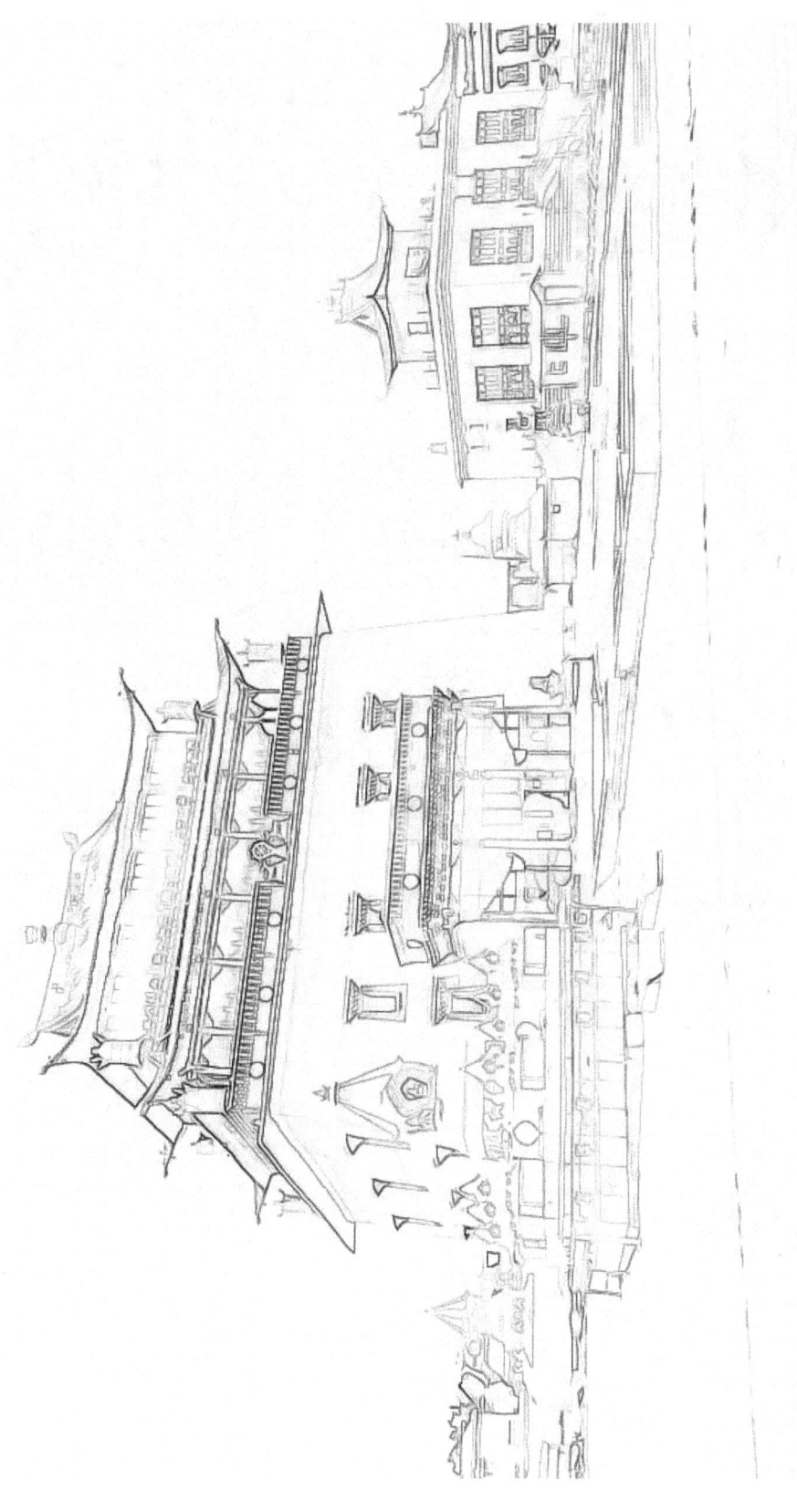

The Gandantegchinlen or Gandan Monastery is a Chinese style Tibetan

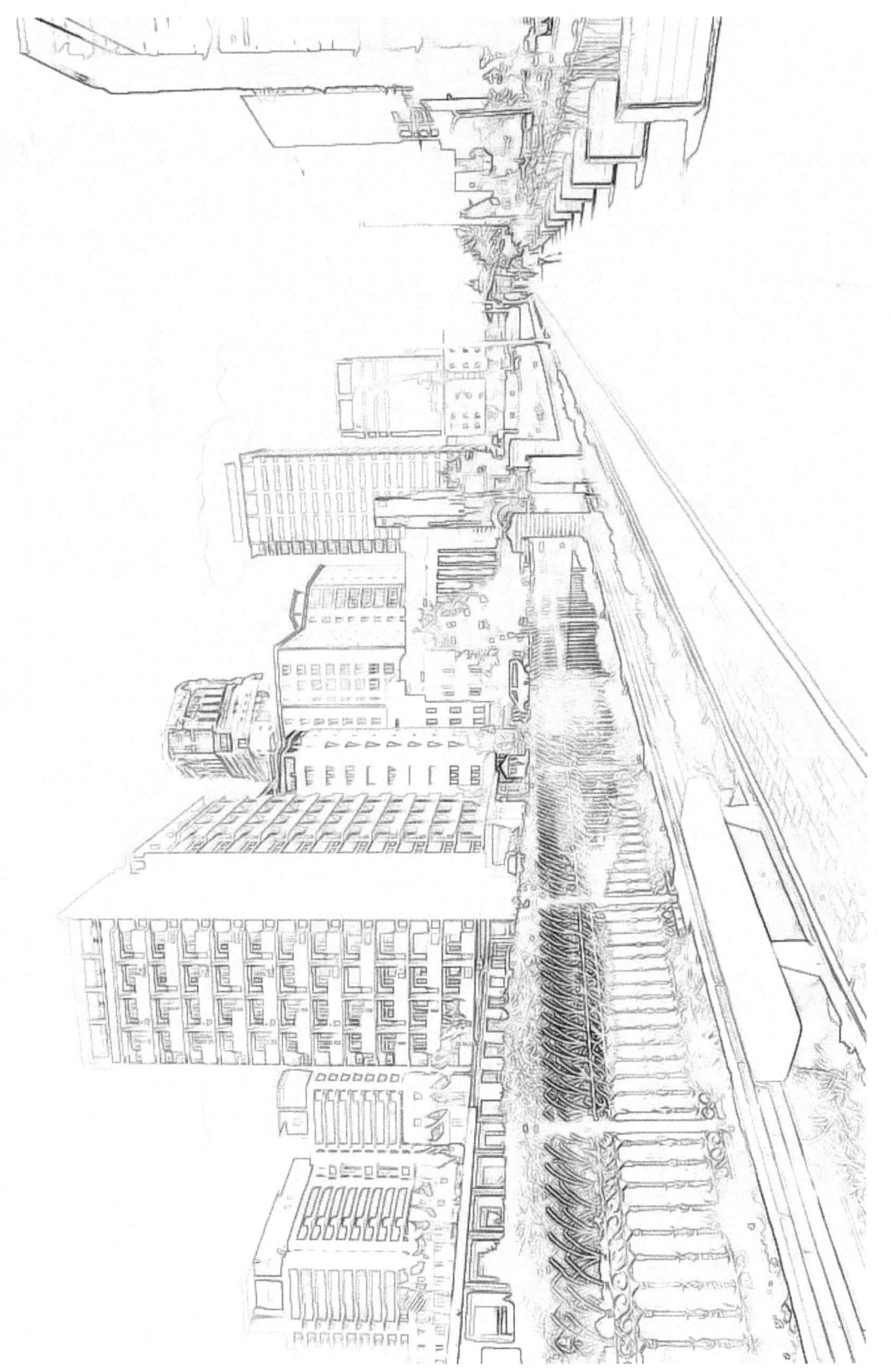

Modern buildings in downtown region of Ulaanbaatar, the capital of Mongolia

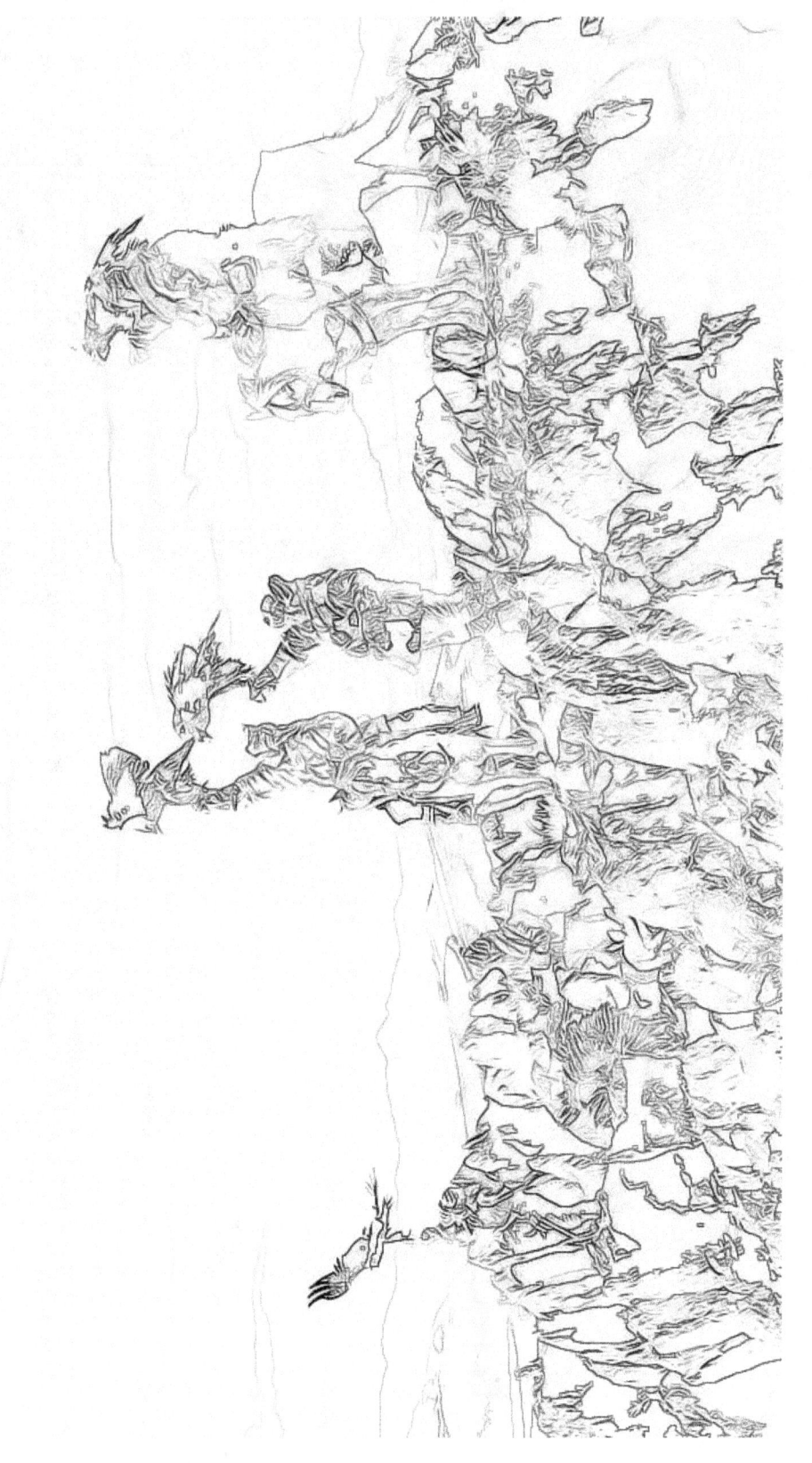

Mongolian eagle Hunters in traditionally wearing typical Mongolian

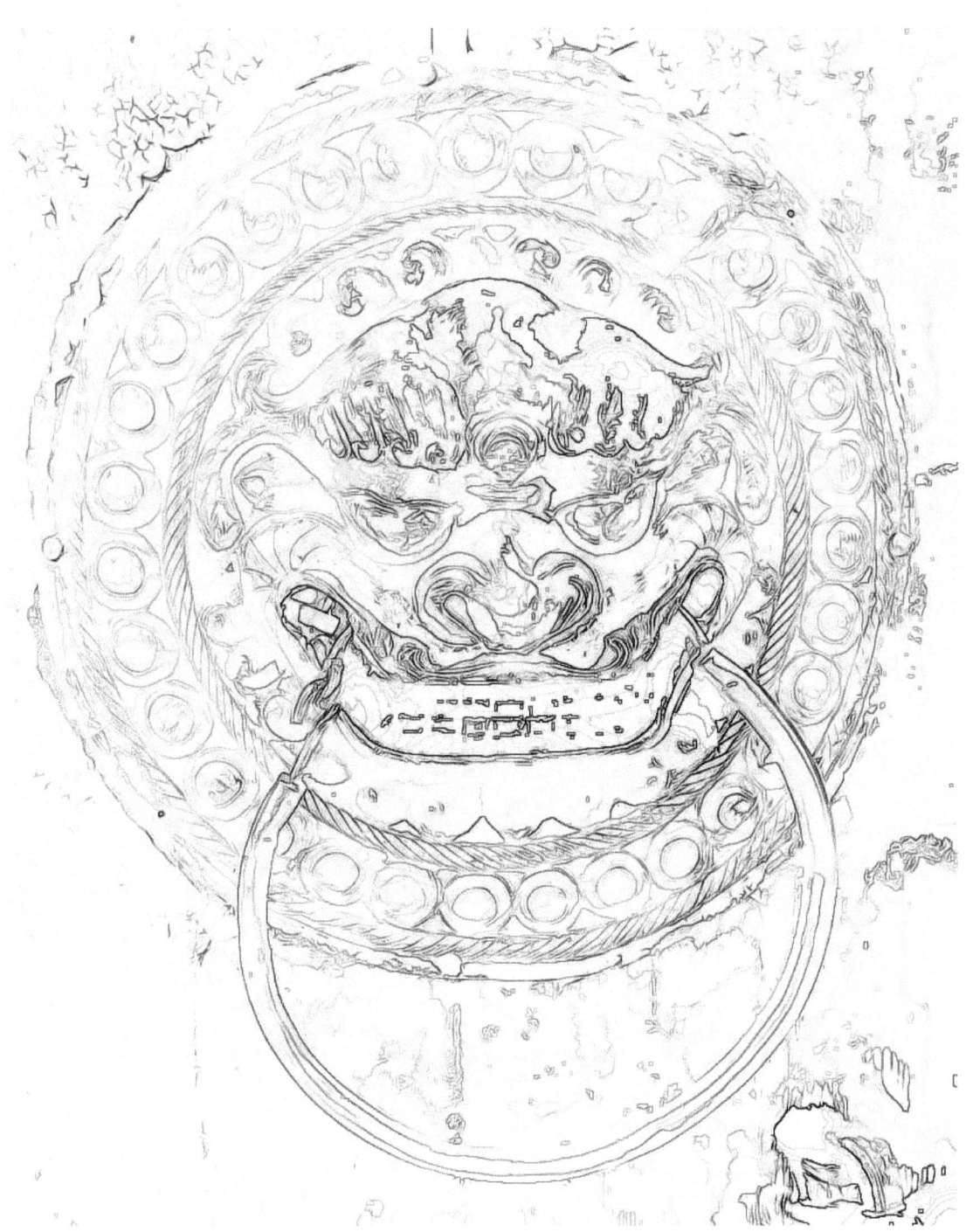

Door knocker Mongolia

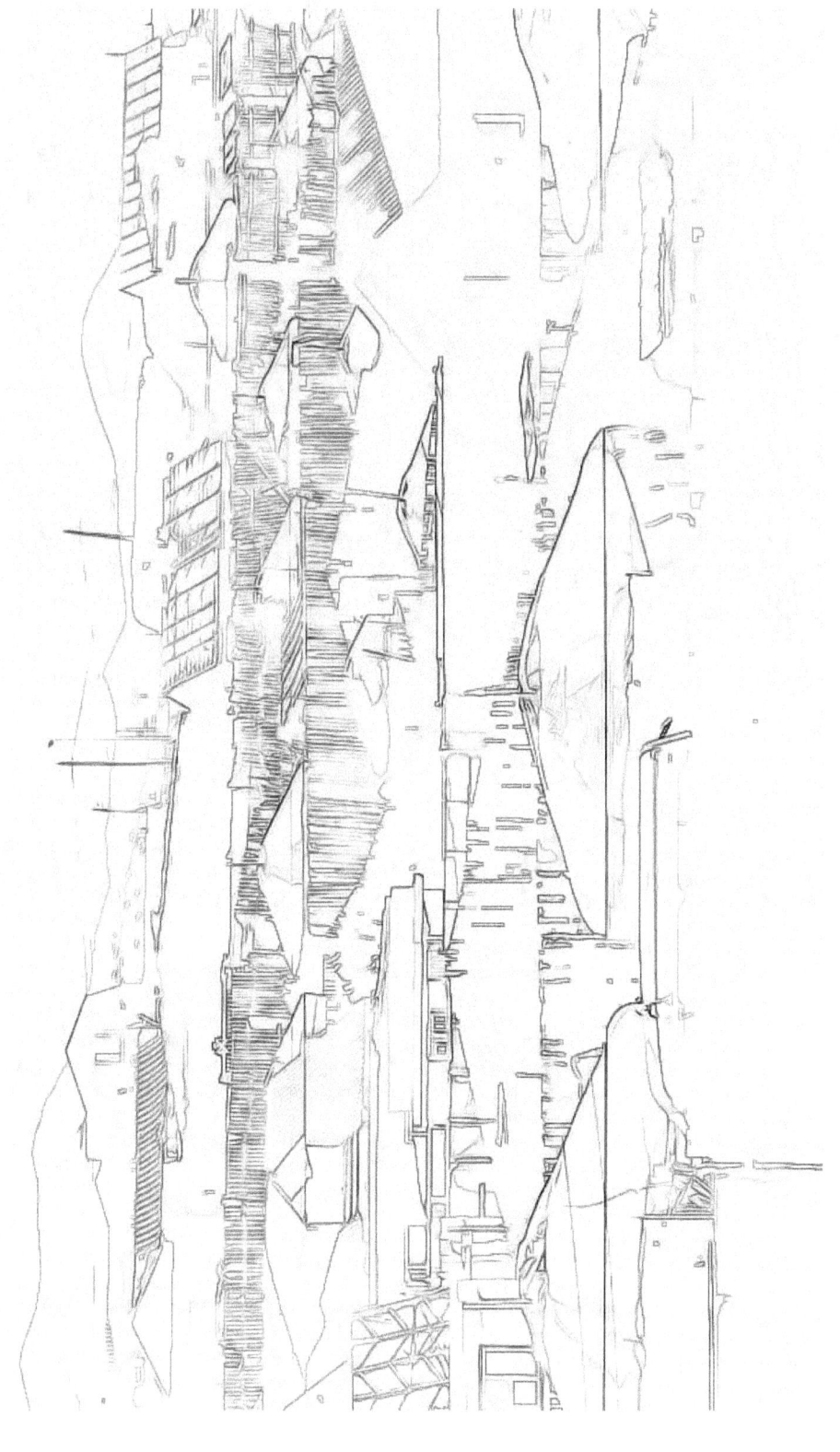

Yurts in the urban area of Ulaanbaatar, Mongolia

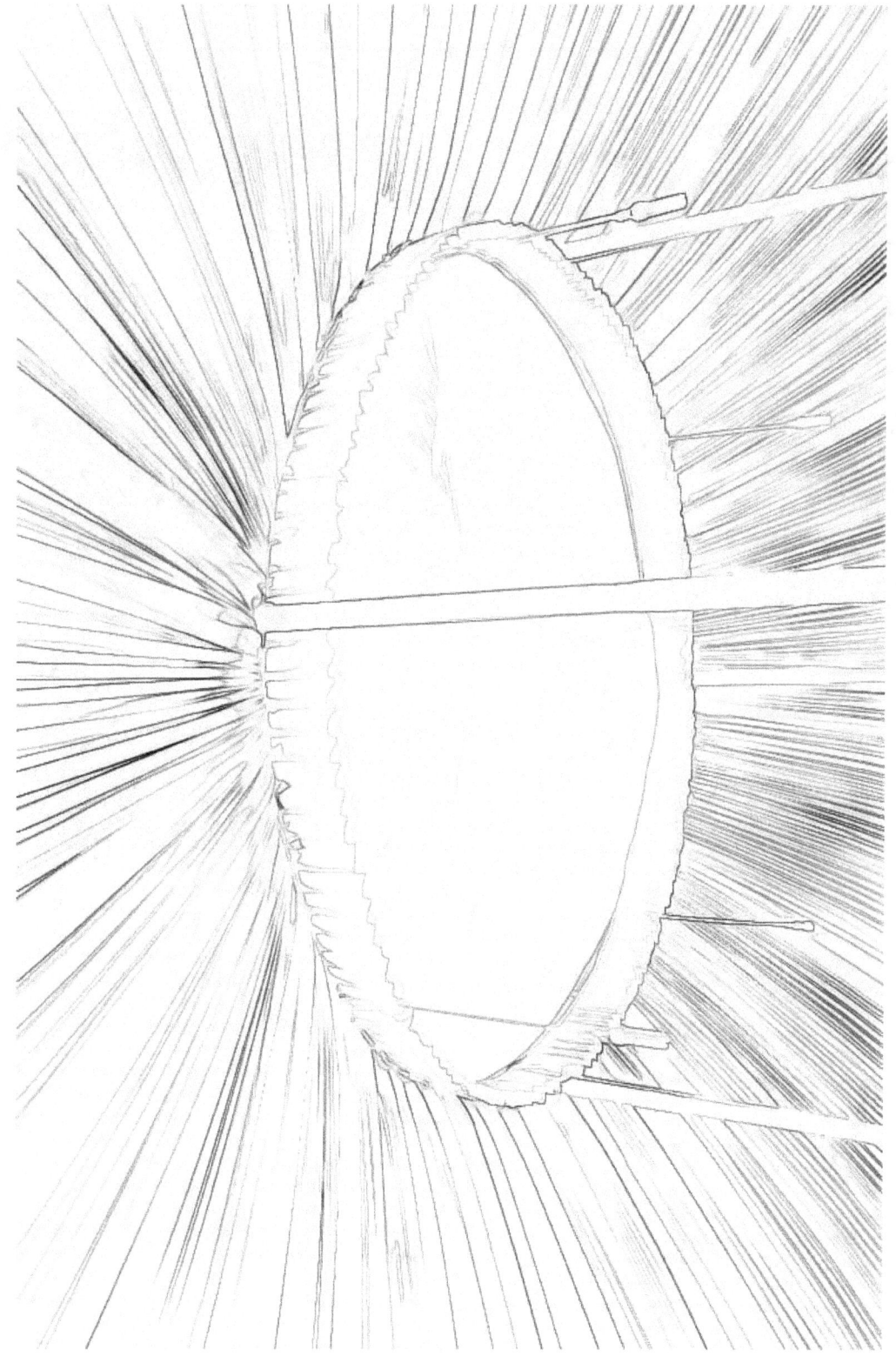

Dome of Mongolia

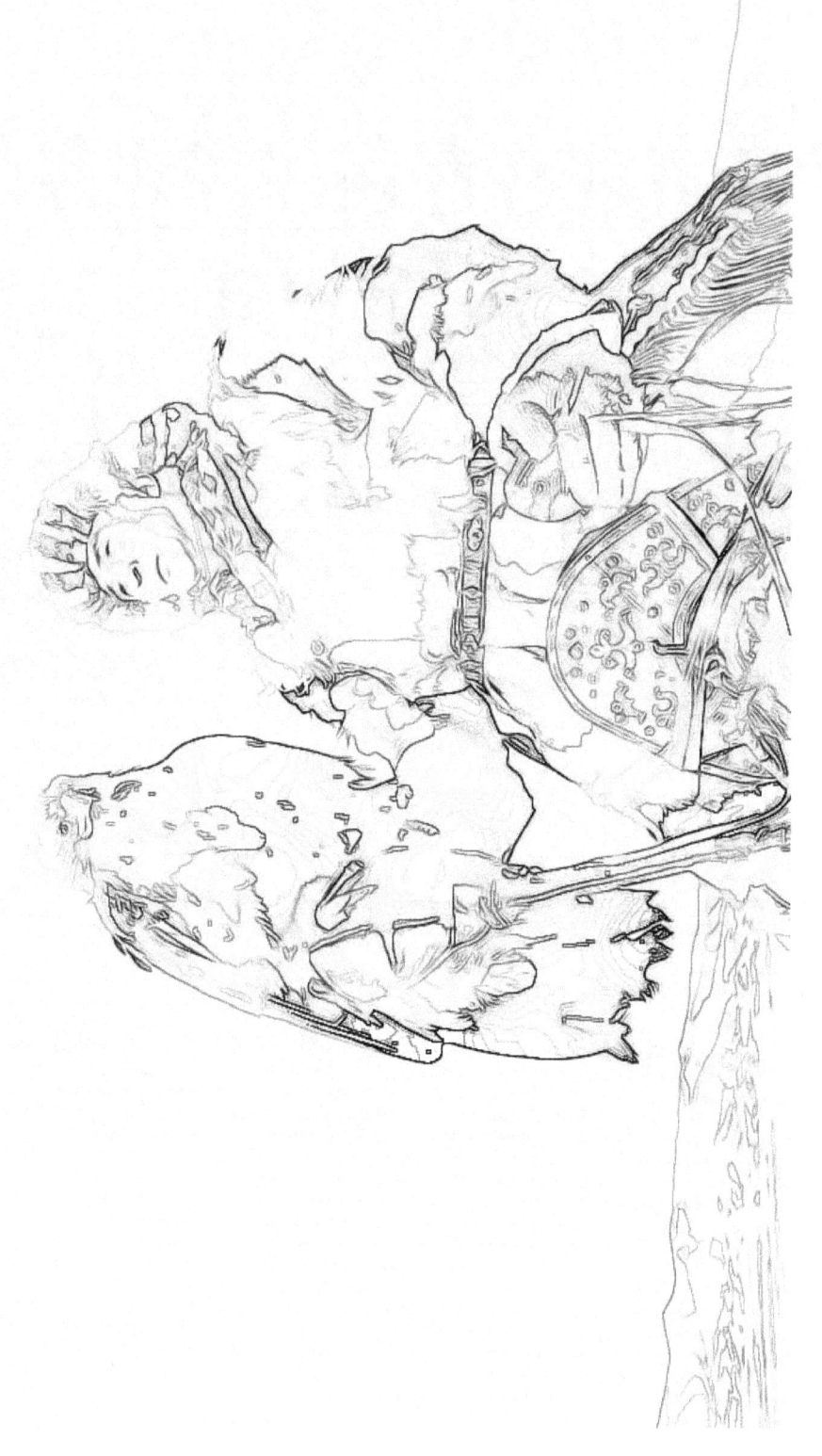

A senior mongolian horseman in traditional kazakh

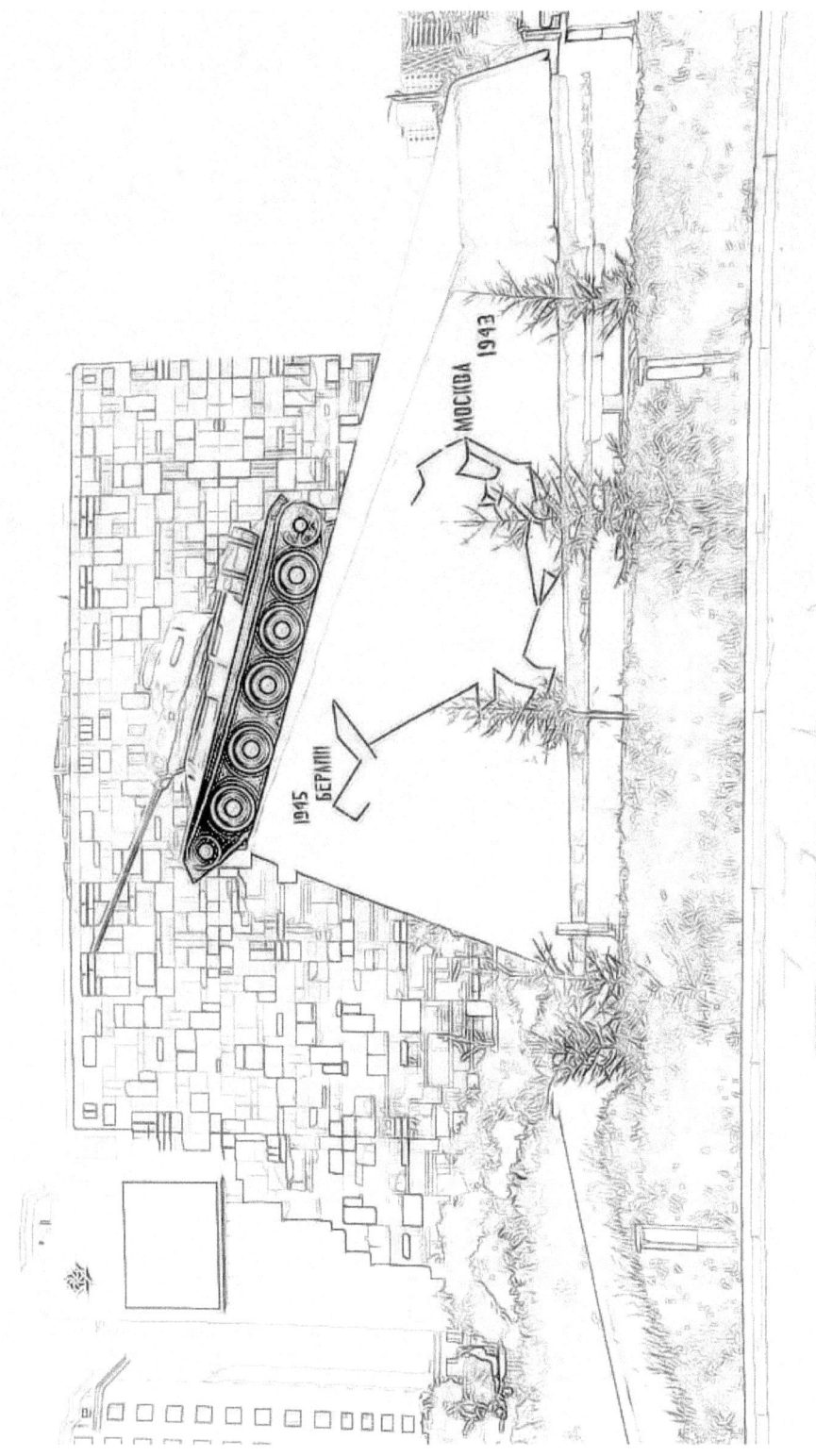

The Zaisan Memorial is a memorial in the Mongolian capital of Ulaanbaatar

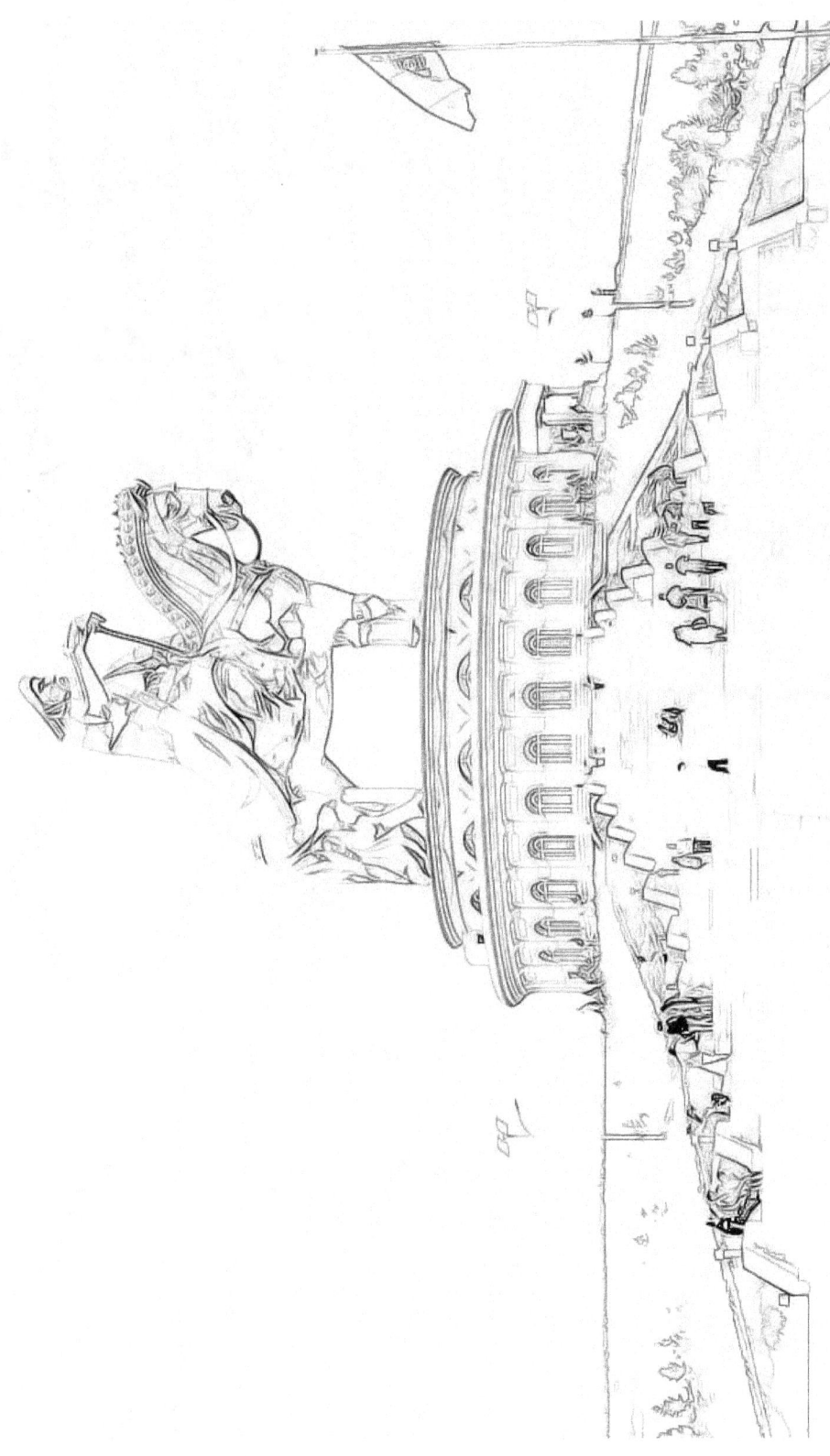

The Genghis Khan Equestrian Statue is a 40 metre tall statue of Genghis Khan

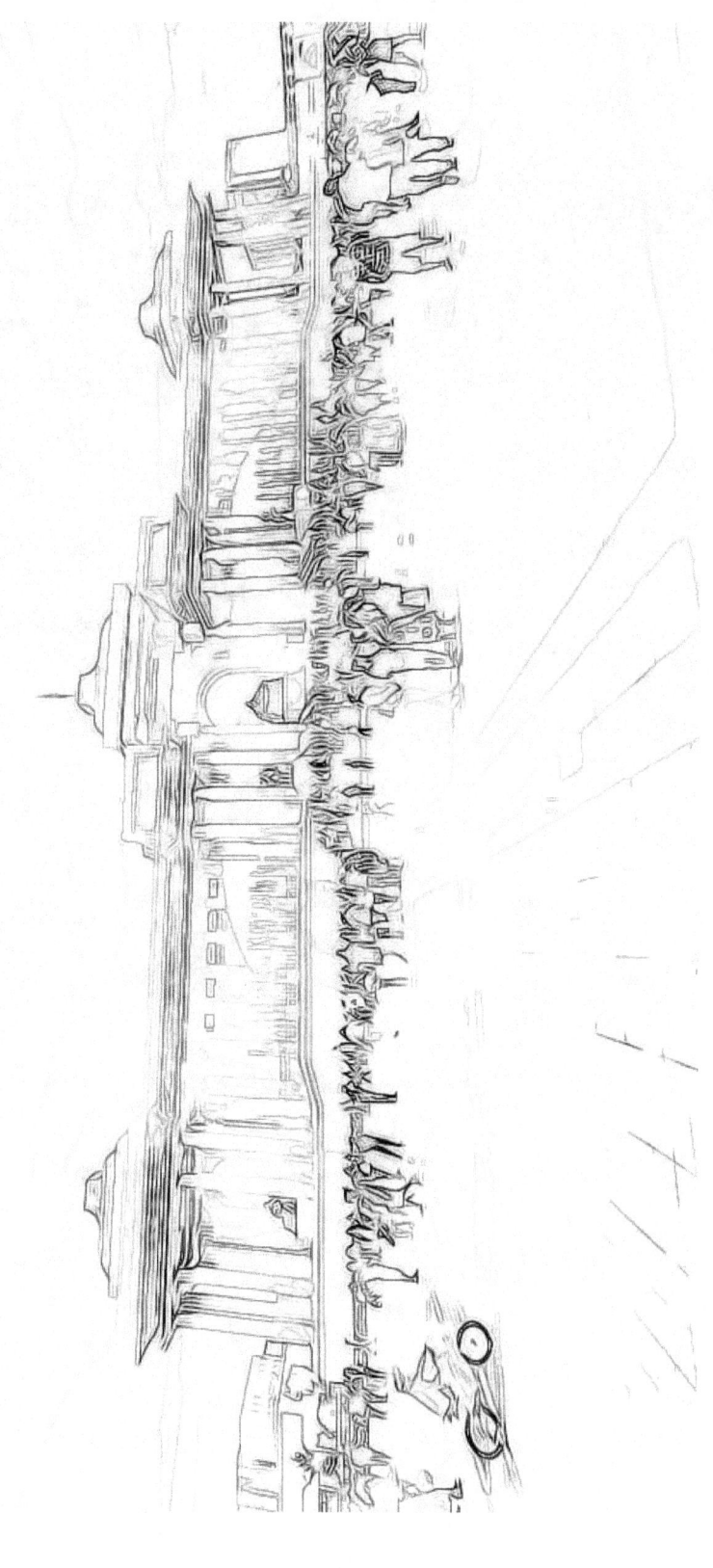

The Government Palace is located on the north side of Chinggis Square

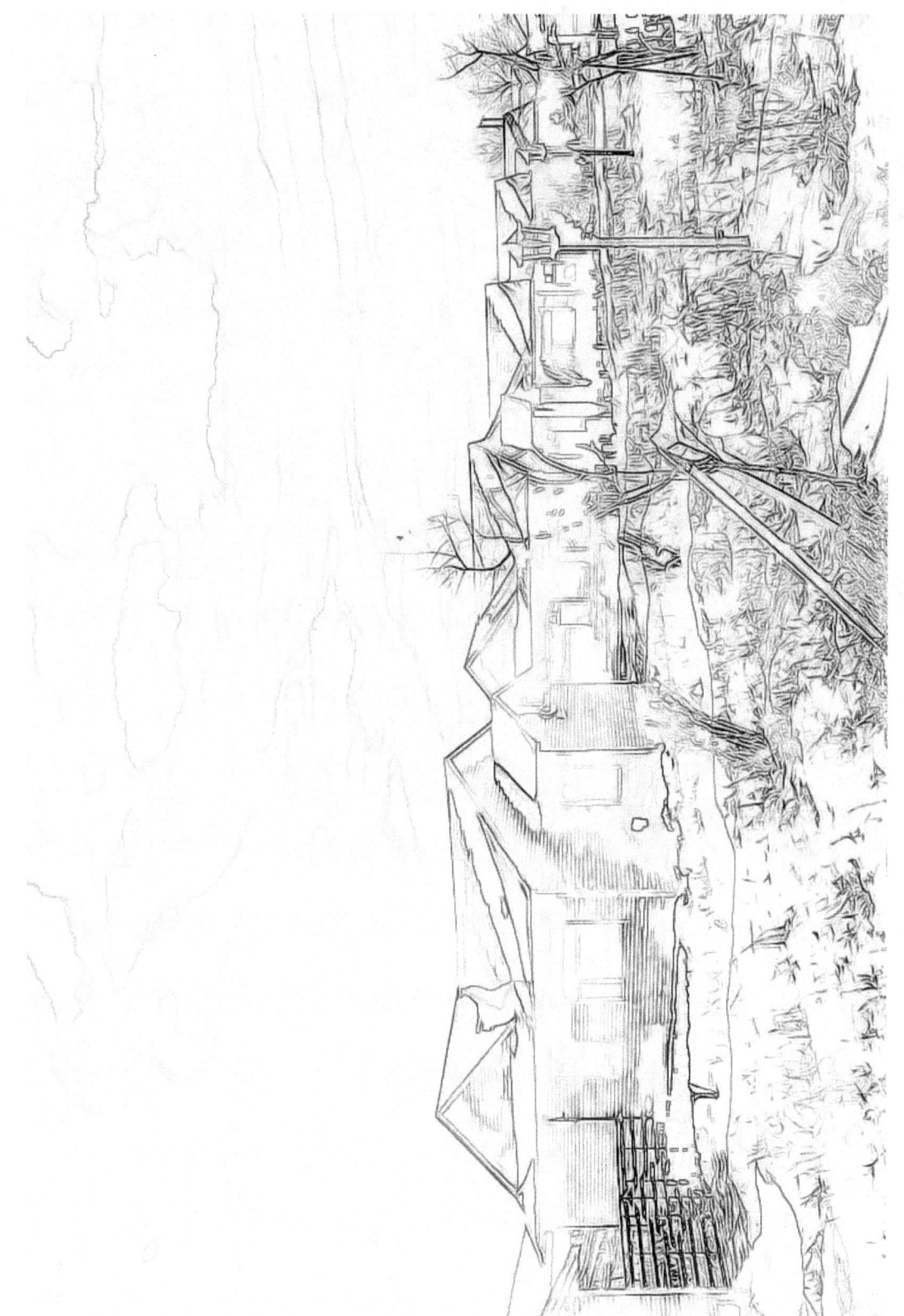

Arxan Resort

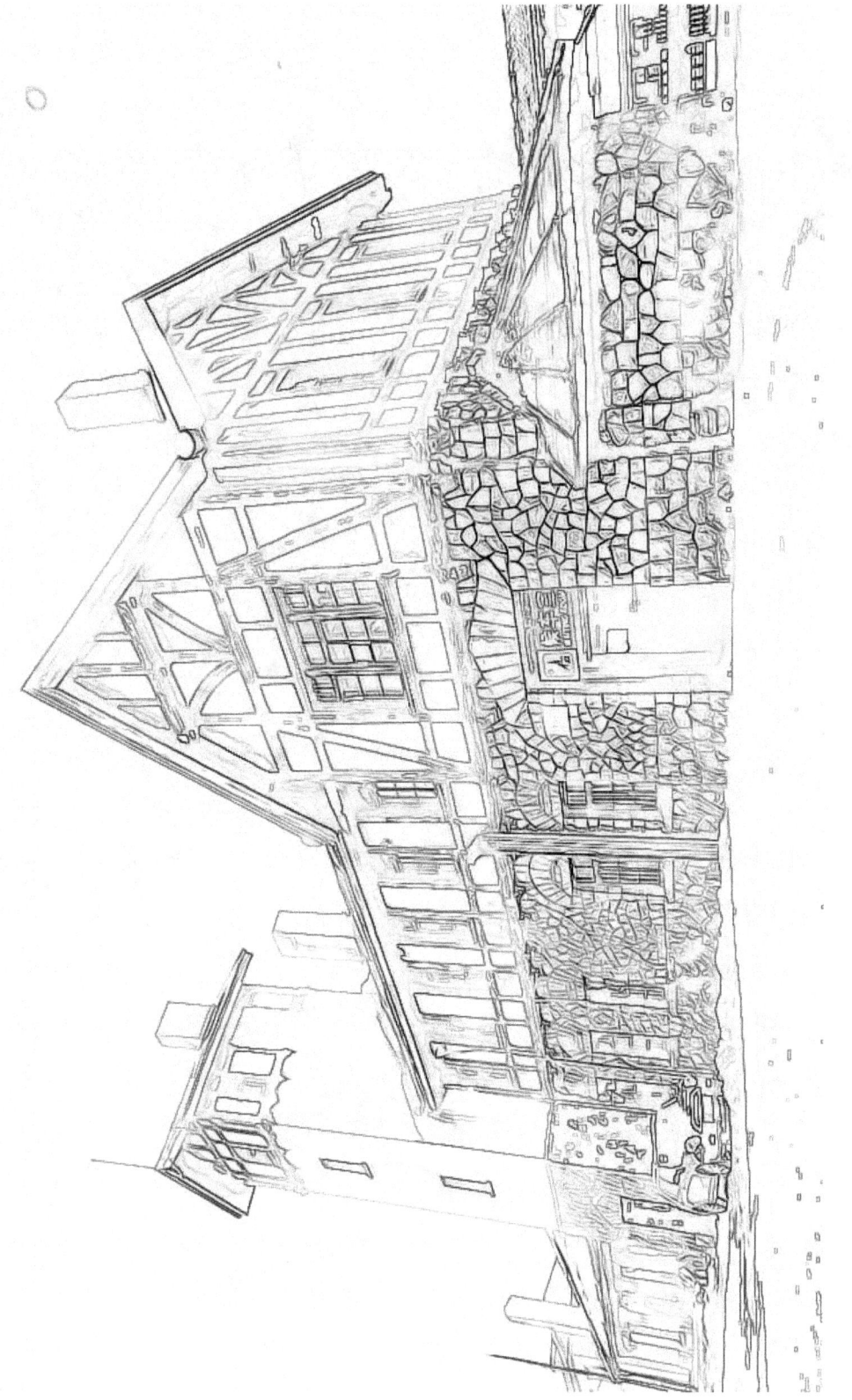

Arxan Railway Station

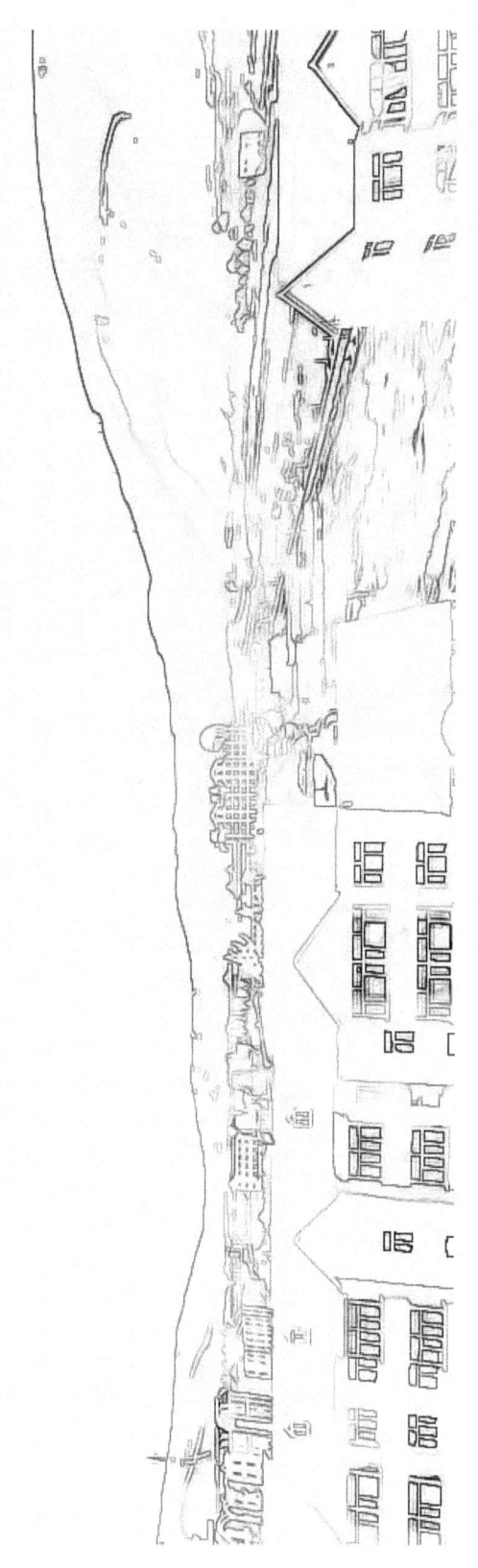

Dawn of Arxan City

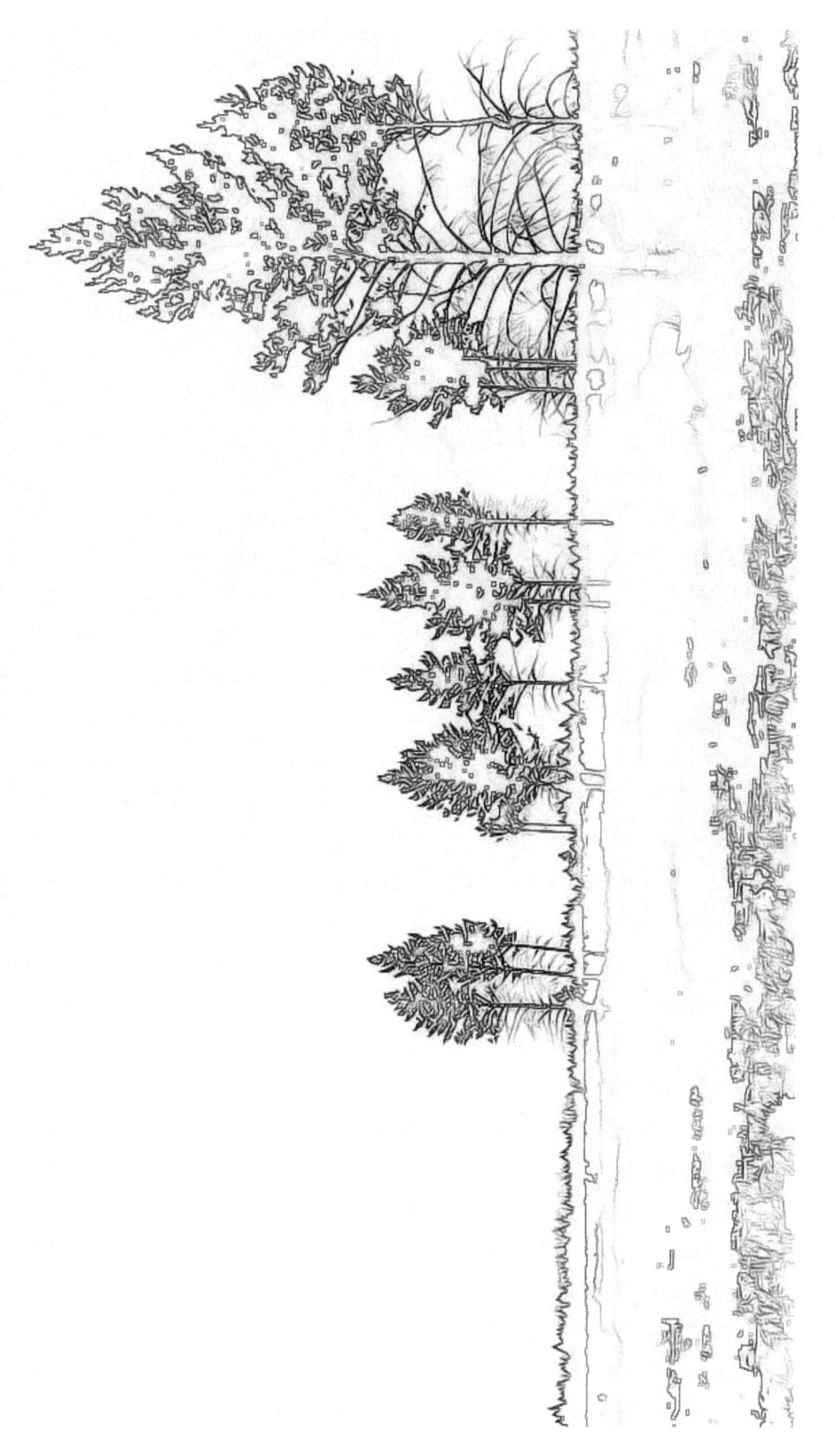

Inner Mongolia beautiful scenery along the way

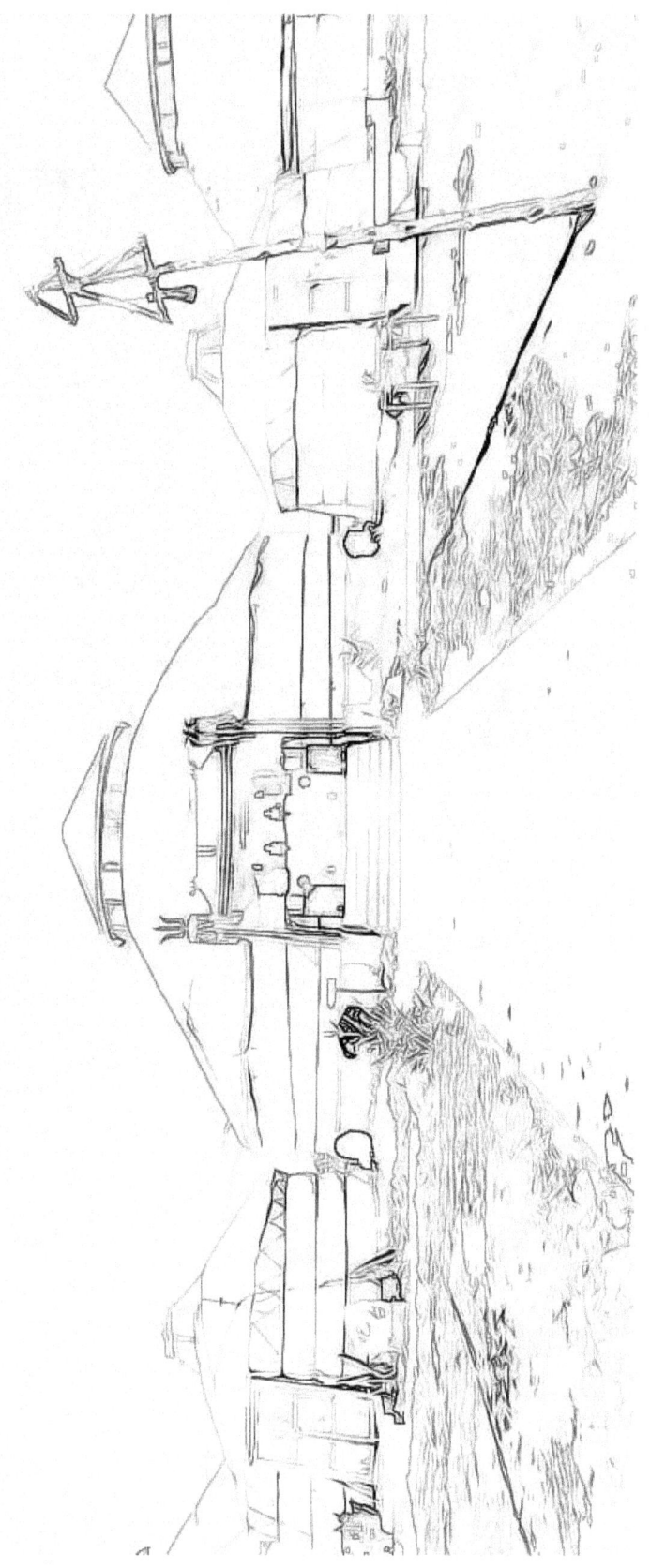

Hailar grassland tribe

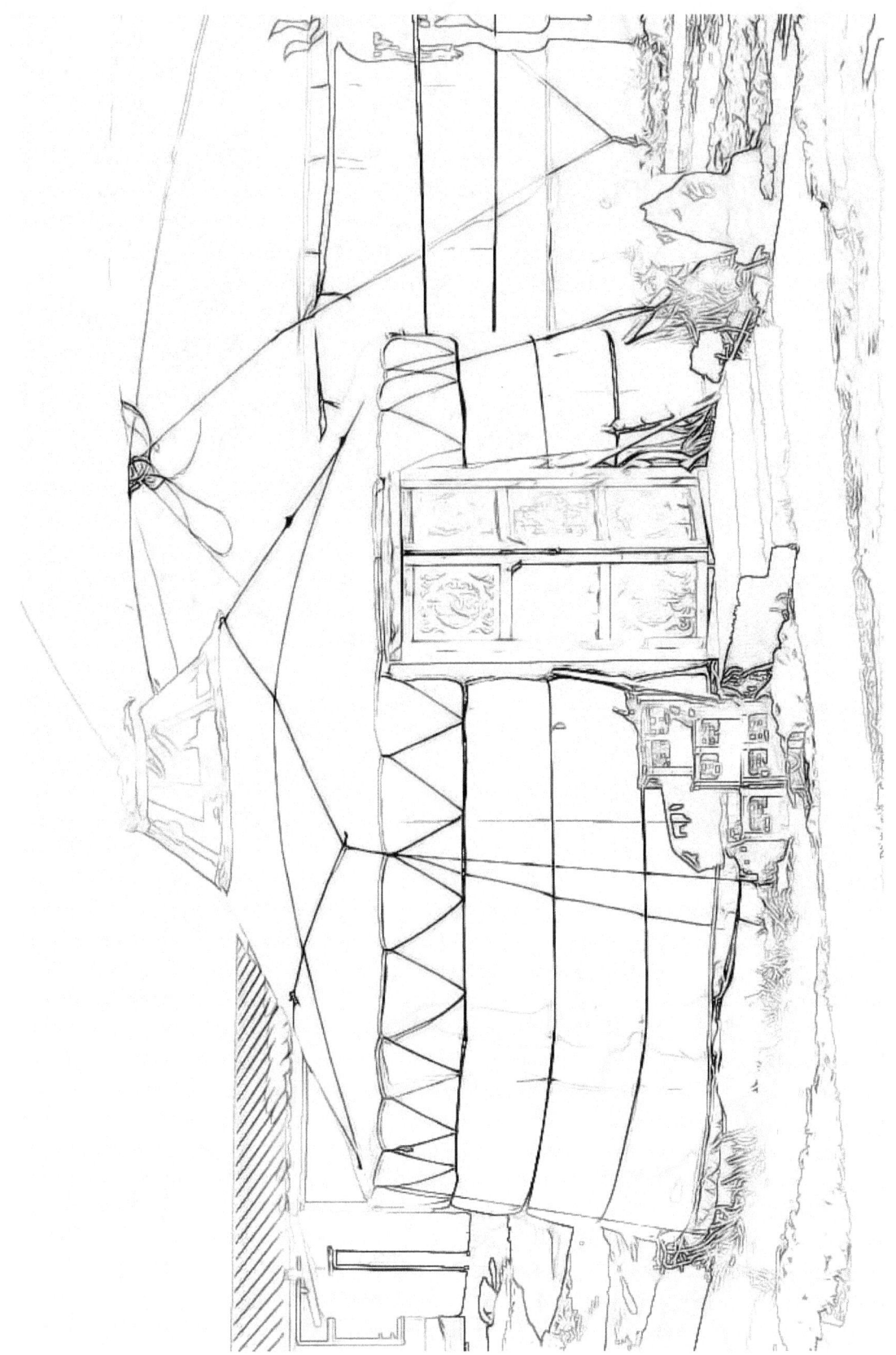

Hailar grassland tribe

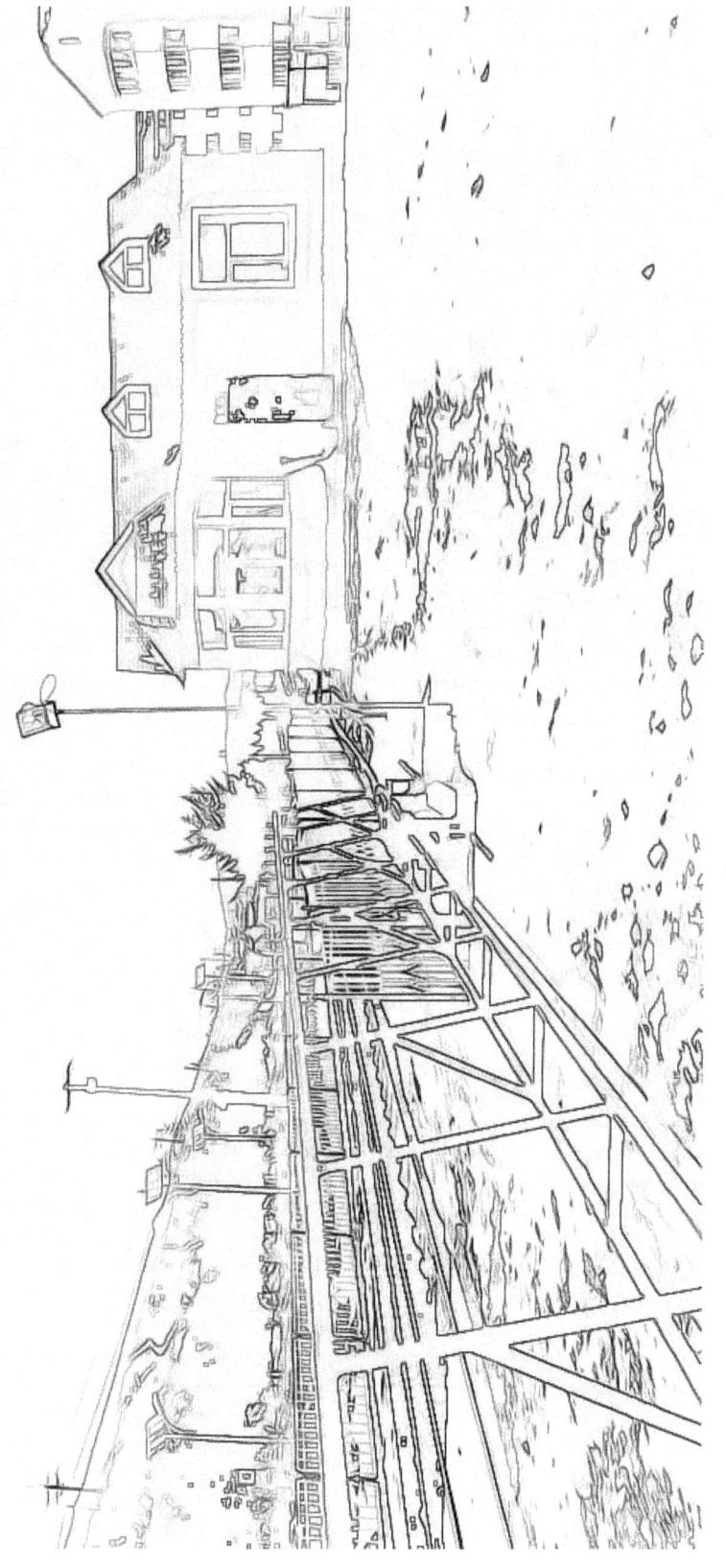

Arxan Railway Station

Picture Guide for this book : http://bit.ly/mongoria_best_2017
Don't Miss Another our Books.

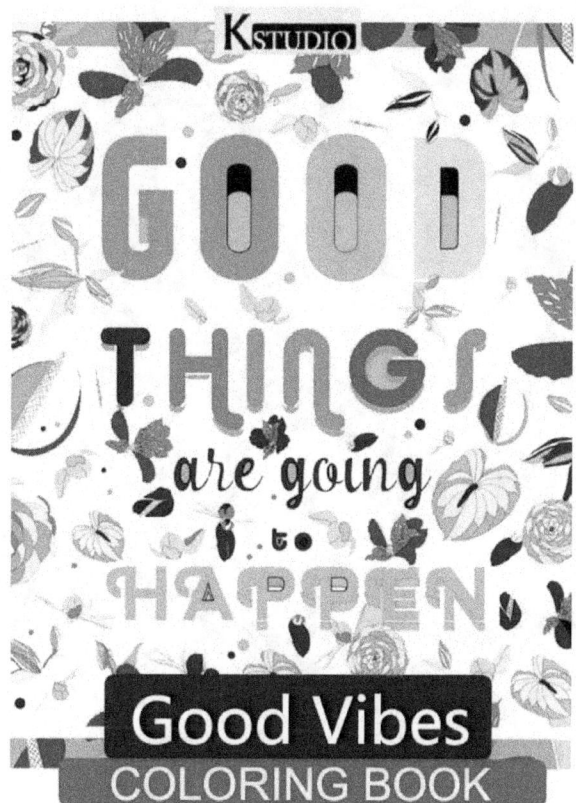

http://bit.ly/good_vibes_1

ISBN : 1530381223
(Use this ISBN for searching on amazon.com)

www.ingramcontent.com/pod-product-compliance
Lightning Source LLC
Chambersburg PA
CBHW081904170526
45167CB00007B/3148